MYTHOLOG

poems

Robley Whitson

books
1995

mythology
by
Robley Whitson

Library of Congress Catalog Card Number

94-062109

International Standard Book Number

1-55605-354-5

QH Books
Cloverdale Corporation
Briston, IN 46507-9460

Printed in the United States of America

Table Of Contents

The Puzzle Woman	1
In a Desert	2
Blueblack Father and Golden Mother	6
The Enchantress	9
Warrior Horse	13
Water Mother	17
Idols	19
Midnight Noon	26
Sun Dog, Moon Dog	30
Rocking	34
The Heart Collector	38
Kali	45
Getting Born	48
Eye Child	50
Sacred Goats	53
Lazarus Again	56
China Girl	61
Tiger Bed	63
The Heedless Monkey	65
The Quick Brown Fox	68
The White Whale	70
After Twilight	78
Earth: Last Day	81
Ragnarök	88
Dreams with Truth	92
The Three of Them	101

for
Kathryn
my near sister

Mytholog

The ancient Australian peoples identified the significance of the mythical with the illuminating image of *Dream Time*—not a once-upon-a-time or an in-the-beginning, but a before-any-beginning when all the first places and people emerged through Dream. We can now recognize the truly creative insight in this archaic image of Dream— now that we realize that dreaming is an integral and critical part of human consciousness.

And we are beginning to realize how gigantic the whole of consciousness is: its awake and asleep states, the multiple deep non-conscious layers, the ways these interrelate and communicate, and ultimately appear in asleep consciousness dreams, then are remembered in awake consciousness in a symbolic language only partially translatable. We dream in symbols and these same symbols become the stuff of myth.

Myth, *mythos*, is simply a story, a story of reality spoken in the language of symbol. And all myths are true stories, but fully true only in their original language of symbol—inevitably distorted when translated into the awake state language of simple nouns and verbs controlled by syntax and logic attempting to reduce the symbols to *a* meaning. But when words are used to carry the symbols and evoke the complex and elusive experience they embody, we are enabled to encounter the *feel* of their truth.

It is only a little more than a century since we began to recognize dreams as another dimension of our own consciousness, rather than as "sendings," intrusions from unknown sources outside us. We have also come to recognize that the symbols in our dreaming have some sort of common base, as they are found in dreams and myths throughout our world. The image facing the title page, from a monumental carving of the ancient Maya, symbolizes transcending the boundary seeming to separate the mortal and immortal spheres: the dark splotches and rows of dots represent sacrificial blood, the plumed serpent is the earth monster which swallows up the dead, the figure emerging from its mouth is the sacred ancestral being evoked by the living who offered their blood. There is a power to penetrate the barrier of death and so bring oracular wisdom to the living:

self-sacrifice – although the specific shaping of the symbols will differ from culture to culture, this Maya myth symbol certainly resonates with Christian sacrifice, with that of the ancient Judaic Temple, with Tibetan Bon rituals, and so many others.

The myths of Dream Time were first spoken-and-heard, in ways that stirred each to recognize: Yes! I experience that too! Remembered and repeated as long as that response kept happening, the form of the speaking is always the dynamic of poetry: metaphor and sound. Poetry dreams myths, and poetry myths dreams (if myth is not a verb, it should be!). Myth-Dreams are also Mysteries, ultimately the unique mystery that so fascinates us: ourselves. The human self which seems so small, indeed insignificant in the context of our unthinkably vast universe, is seen as truly unlimited in the mystery of myth-dreams. In our mything we relate absolutely everything to our sense of self – who *we* are and what *it* is, significant together – creatively, destructively, in fact, in every way.

Most mysteriously, the sense of self can be experienced as breaking through into the ultimate Transcendence, illogical though that seems to the narrow-band of awake state thinking!(The Hindu Brahman-atman convertibility, the Buddhist No-self and Buddha-nature paradox in the East, in the West the Christian rising through death into the eternal life of Divine Existence, the Judaic Kabalist entry into the Shekinah, and many others.)

The poems of this *Mytholog* arise in the Dream Time of one self. The first nine are myths of beginnings, of maleness and femaleness (one to another, and internally within anyone), and of primordial response to Mystery. The next three (Rocking, The Heart Collector, Kali) shift to a story form of the great puzzle embedded in the urge to immortality. The eight poems following are actual family history stories of kith-and-kin. The final six approach the edge of experience: endings and transformations. The last poem, The Three of Them, leaves unanswered, as it must, who this "other" of us is that makes possible all our dreaming and mything, the Puzzle Pieces dropped into our Dream Time lives.

The Puzzle Woman

Every winter afternoon late
she shadows down the westward hillside
to pick through leftover day scraps.
Thin and ancient–
so she seems to any who bother to see her–
she is sunset young, moonrise old,
and thin as only starlight is
filled with emptied space.
Spider thread hair rambles aimlessly
while the black centers of her eyes
search out dark spots and splotches,
to discover which ones do not grow
as light fades,
to make them into midnight signs.

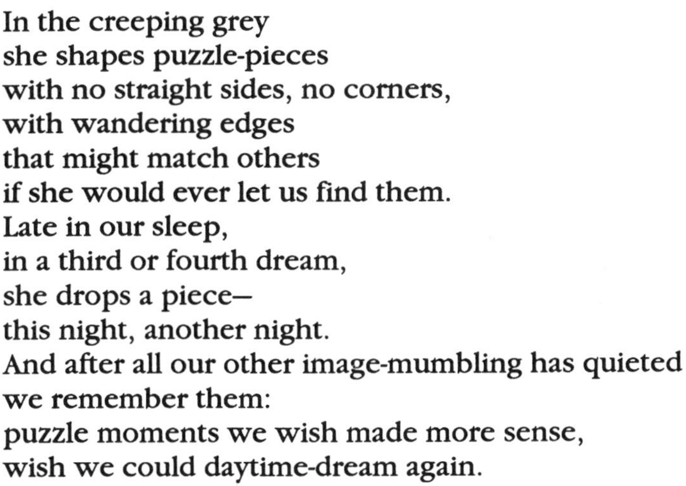

In the creeping grey
she shapes puzzle-pieces
with no straight sides, no corners,
with wandering edges
that might match others
if she would ever let us find them.
Late in our sleep,
in a third or fourth dream,
she drops a piece–
this night, another night.
And after all our other image-mumbling has quieted
we remember them:
puzzle moments we wish made more sense,
wish we could daytime-dream again.

We wonder why she does it,
gives just fragments
and only while we sleep.
I wonder how to find the someone
with midnight sign puzzle-pieces matching mine.
In a next dream we might meet.
Then the two of us will wonder,
or we two shall know.

In a Desert

Lines of horizon haze
laid on in blurs
in hovers
over sandpaper flats
peppered with weed–
haze almost in color,
almost a blue
if hot sky turns blue,
almost a tan
if desert dust
ever stops shivering.
Lines where everything is long
long enough to stretch
end around nearly to end
to the spot where
a low slung sun
blots the circle.

———

You can see the haze,
almost see through it–
not smell it, though.
Far too far away
even if you walked
there forever–
which is what we do
all the time anyway,
walking the lines of light
our eyes speed along
faster than our feet
can go or want to.

So we will be able
to keep from catching
what we think we see
might be adrift behind the haze
we cannot smell.

———

Our feet
the one, the other
one, other
each for a step-moment
flat on the sand
lifted, put down
as we go there
through the heat
towards the blur.

We do not hover over
anywhere.
We are always there,
clear and salty
in our evaporating skins.
The hovering is up and ahead
where we are going
by flat-footed steps,
always right here
or just here
in the splayed line
trailing back behind
forgetting.

———

After a while we know
the idea-of-a-color
is what we must have—
not any one color
but what color can be
once it is inside us.
What color the mind is,
or the color our fingertips
feel when they touch something.

The sky can be blue
or red or black or any,
inside my mind.
The dust can feel like
any sky color I want
because I can touch the grains
if I want.
So the haze can be
almost blue
almost tan.
What I want.

When I do touch it
I know why desert dust
never stops shivering:
in among all the grains
I can feel a color—
all bits of people
hidden in the grit.

They and mountains erode
together into a place
where we walk in footsteps,
where the heated air
makes our eyes shimmer
and glare-over with tears
we cannot afford
dry in the desert.

The color of them all
fingering inside my mind
is what turns everything
into layers, and
into lines, long lines, and
into... just: into.
Only the sun stops it,
blinds out their circling,
frees us for a while
from all this walking
which nevertheless
goes on and on
even when we stop
because of the sun.

A sun exploding,
flares in white fire
white but whiter-whiter,
though so far away out there,
even farther away than I am—
exploding inaudible spume
too bright for colors—
except for the Silent colors.
Any color I want.

Blueblack Father and Golden Mother

The blueblack man
stands naked
in the slant of shade.
        The golden woman
        glows with sunskin
        warm against water.

The ivory bowl
holds him in
easily balanced on restless legs.
Line of spine and neck,
straight slope of shoulders
slung with arms and hands
heavy muscle woven,
are the memory of the push and pull
which worked stone and earth
into all their massy shapes.

        She casts no shadows
        as rounds swerve to meet
        then merge into one another
        without line or crease,
        bone all but hidden
        under soft folds
        covering flesh converging.
        Swell and curve,
        fall and hollow
        are all alight.

The blueblack skin
stretches over braided thighs
up to their sphering together,
stretches over layered slabs of back,
the near-square bulges of chest,
the triple belted trunk,

the knotted interlock of flanks.
Blueblack hoods his head
and masks his face
so only opened eyes
are the stars in his night.

Clothed in golden white,
the pulse beneath
suggests its tint—
the blood whose tide
sweeps life in and out.
The rises and slopes,
the wanderings of surface
over mounds and down
into deeps within,
are the flow-ways
drawing dark to touch.

He steps from shade into sun,
down from shore into pool,
and slowly enters the water
without ripple circle,
without sound.
All his might melts away
as he leans back
into quiet—
once.

She laughs and laughs.
She splashes that whole wet world
into a universe of drops
that catch at her white light
and spray it out all in color.
And she cries with glee—
See!
gold and white and blue and black,
all wild in the water!

Then he stands and waits for her,
the stars in his night face
open to her.
And the pool grows calm
as the sun slowly lies down
into the touch of the water.

She comes close—
walking half swimming,
the surface shimmering out from her,
lapping up against him—
the flicker of bright oceans
flashed all over his skin.

From these two have come forth
all the gleaming bronze generations,
who have traveled out into every world
and filled them with their life.

Every night when it is darkest
some look up into the sky,
searching the numberless stars
for the two eyes of our blueblack father.
Every day when light reaches everywhere
some look up to the sun,
squinting against the dazzle
for the shadowless glow of our golden mother.

We love the quiet of still water.
We laugh as we splash it
into all its spray of colors.
We stare at the glint of waves
cast up on shadow-dark rock or tree.

The Enchantress

1
She feels rain
inside her skin
just where the blood begins–
    rain misting into half-dreams,
    rain pelting stinging nerves,
    rain flow-washing rough life.

She lies lazy,
stretched out
curved over everywhere,
the earth beneath her,
all breathing within her.

She is Power:
    every embrace
    even ones made grab-ugly,
    every touch
    every need to touch, be touched
    especially the sad ignored.

Everything hard and sharp
she rounds and softens
into infants
born dying.

She sings her wordless songs
to the boychild–
who hears
    the rise and fall of sound
    the rush of rhythms,
    but knows no meanings.

She speaks her songless words
to the girlchild–
who knows
    secret binding spells
    puzzles bonding,
    but hears no humming.

In the light
she sings her wordless songs.
At night
she whispers silent words.

2
In light at night
their shadows merge
in undivision
invisible.
Not sleeping, not stirring
each hears the slow beat of heart,
a far away tread
wandering through radiating veins.
Each feels that beat
pulsing through flesh against flesh.

Face turned to face and beyond,
so each seeing opposite
around the curve of night
into blue sun gold
horizons away,
curved around again and back
into each other in the dark–
holding and held
in their world of only two,
the warm center
of the circle world of sun
of the spiral world of stars–
receiving and received.

She whispers when he sings
his man-moan moments
where he can feel only himself,
think of nothing
picture no one,
eyes pinched tight
against anything else existing—
the explosion creating himself
as his own new universe,
pleasure pain drained
to drift away into dust sleep.

He can learn to listen
to his fade away echo,
and there overhear her
as she whispers her words.
He can look into the dark
with the black centers of his eyes
full open, deep absorbing.

3
Your rib fingers
undulating
with breath-soft
separations invitations
to my hand fingers
to rest together
interlaced spaced
upon your breathing.

Your breath
held warm in my hand—
I must not try
to grasp it
as it slips away
through closing fingers.

You breathe it out
giving yourself away
into open fingers
not grasping
but molding themselves to you.

You breathe in
they spread as you grow,
you breathe out
they feel the lessening
of becoming gift.
When you sleep
I listen within you
hearing my wordless song.
I whisper with you
then watch your waking eyes
to see you grow to know
who I really am—
until the night your dream
sings the words aloud at last
and there is no waking,
then my chanting ends
and my spell binds
our now
all ways.

Warrior Horse

1
Moon-white and naked
astride a snow wind stallion–
hard thighs tight around flanks
whose arched bones
span the beast chest
and spread with every breath.
The grip of his legs
pulls in the gallop plunge
and his whole trunk
thuds with the hammering–
stones chipped, powder dust
kicked up to haze the air.

The man skin
the horse hide
do more than touch.
They are almost one surface
of a single creature
contrived a hundred centuries ago
when the first madman
jumped up upon a back
that reared in terror,
every nerve bucking
to thrash off a killer.
But there were no claws
digging in clinging,
no jaws snapping the life neck.
There were hands grasping,
chest and belly pressing forward,
legs scrambling to hold.

The feel of skin and hide
shudded into a new creation:
    hooves and feet and hands,
     heads and breaths and hearts–
two now separable side by side
yet two now become one,
one moving in power.

2
They ride to a war
with no battles,
no attacking foes,
nothing to pillage,
no one to rape.
It is war raged within,
the struggle to break free,
to be free,
to become the one who is free–
freed from things,
everything,
    the things we wrap around us,
    the disguises we put on
so others will not know
who we really are.

That first madman
on the last wild horse–
the dumb beast accepted him
by the feel of him,
by skin on hide,
by the heft of flesh.
Warriors ride naked,
naked as horses,
covered with no thing,
protected by no thing–
free triumphant to be
the wonder each is.

3

Man-horse travels the earth
away from all the lands
with all their things
until at the end of the world
where forest thins toward shore
man and horse come apart,
the stallion roaming off
to find another called to fight,
his warrior going to the sea
sounding beyond the trees.

He walks through branch shadows
that tiger stripe him
up and down his legs
with their swell of shifting balances,
up across triangles and squares,
firm folds and soft ridges,
all flooding and ebbing
with every quiet stride.

The world is suddenly simpler:
    sea, sand, sky.
The dazzle heat slicks him,
flashed sun silk binds him,
and he sleeps a final dream–
of the rise and fall of tides,
the rhythms of waves;
of the shimmer glow of someone,
    someone there
at the curve of the water;
of both together
in the taut string
of the ocean bow-horizon–
    then gone,
beyond earth and sun
and all worlds of suns.

Their star stung skins
open pore mouths wide
to feast upon each other
drawing each other in,
skin into skin—
then gone
into one.

4

Across the light ages
on a once remembered earth
another young warrior
moon-white and naked
mounts the snow wind stallion
to ride to his war.
From the far outside
of all that seems to be,
a momentary spark
ticks his eye
and his thighs sense
pleasure shiver through the horse.

Shining through the blank of sky
the spark marks the stallion eye:
two more of mine are one,
and now one with all the others,
all free in That One.

The warrior astride,
the steed moving in power
into war always already won—
the prance of the beast is proud.

Water Mother

I remember the pond
where they found her,
floating
face up sunsmiling,
hair trailing wet
tangled in the reeds.

How fearful they were
fishing her out–
what would it feel like,
the touch of her,
cold in the water?...
who would free her hair?
Then their terror:
she still lived,
alive but unmoving;
soft hum in her smile,
she still breathed.

They carried her home,
laid her in the great bed,
left her sleeping.
Everyone who touched her
that first time
would have to die.
But the bold one
who pulled her hair
from its grasp on the reeds
lived on and on,
old in her silence.

When she woke
it was to him,
drawing him to her,
into her.
Without a sound
she shaped a girlchild,
and slowly each day
removed whatever was his
from the swelling within her:
the girlchild would be hers,
wholly hers—
just as the silence was hers,
his old silence.

For the day of the birthing
they returned to the pond,
and the infant swam out of her
in among the reeds.
Every end of day
the old man came to watch
as her child grew
girl to woman,
her tendril hair
slipping among reed stalks
until that time
when he would call the men,
the ever-forgetful men,
to fish her out,
then see the new bold one
take hold of her hair
and fall quiet.

I remember the pond:
bold young men
fingering the floating hair;
all of us grown silent,
never forgetful
of the sunsmiling faces.

Idols

ONE

The two ravens fly ahead—
the black of night beyond day
beyond twilight,
the black of night before day
before dawnlight.
They cry out
the raw sounds of warning
deep inside our sleep
as we dream a daytime
filled with images that fall
up into our eyes.
The ravens caw call to each other
as they circle around us,
wheel over our waving hands,
then far ahead again
wing us down
down so awkwardly
into our inner dark.

TWO

They wander sunward
ever wanting
never sure
        the five of them
        alive in the spread
        fingers of a hand
always ready to reach
into the deep of sleep
to seize some woman.

They mold her softened bones
into ivory images
with surprise-wide eyes,
send these flying out
to find their way into temples
and there stand behind the altar lamps.

They stare through the flames
at the flickering worshippers
who dare not stare back.

Ivory bone eyes burn
round, dark and empty,
each filled with fire
waiting for a madman
to look up from chanted prayers
into their reflected glare.

They wait, patiently wait,
sputtering the lamplight
but all are always too afraid.

Through moons and stars
they watch for him–
he must kneel there one day.

Ah, good! Now! Here he is–
But–unafraid, unawed–
The fool, the fool is laughing!

Lunatic grin across his mouth,
the shape of words,
soundless smirking words–
He knows! Oh, he knows!

THREE

The sanctuary is lightless,
only the glow
of thin seam-lines
squares the doors,
hints at the rising round of moon
enclosed in the world outside.

The two of them there
alone in the Sacred Dark
where no others dare,
the two of them at full flood
into each other–
his sweat, her blood
mar the marble floor,
a blotch stained forever
into pores of the stone.

Priests come at dawn
to open the doors to the sun:
the two are there
just within the threshold
side by side standing rock-still,
their faces and bodies blurred
into everyman, everywoman,
eroded by the sand and rains
of the thousand years
that are as one night
in the courts of the Most High.

FOUR

She stands on the shore
turned away from the seas,
her feet deep in the sand
that swirls in the surf
then scoops around
curved with the tide.
When waves roll high
she grows tall with them.
When they subside in calm
she falls to mere human size.

She is as old as the oceans
from which she came
when she first led fish
out of the waters
into invisible air.
But she must stay
within the spray and spume
to take them all
one by one.

She always looks landward
scanning the dunes and beyond
for the lines of pilgrims
who travel from shrine to shrine
among the temple cities.
They all stop here,
shave their heads
and give their hair to her.

She gathers their offering
and mats it with mist
into salt-grained cloth
that flaps around her
so they cannot see
her flotsam body

wrapped in smell-foam skin
greened with bits of weed.
They must always fear her:
she brought them forth
and cannot lead them back,
but she will kill them all,
each, one day or night.

They can only hope
their gift of hair
will spare their heads
for another turn of time
from the two sharp swords
she holds crossed before her.
She looks at each one
through the four angles
she forms with the blades,
up and down,
right and left,
to see which heads
will be cut this year–
perhaps the one held pride high,
or that humbled one bowed low,
the smirking face on this side,
or the dull unthinking on the other.

One day through the splash of surf
someone unseen comes up behind her
and snatches off the salt hair cloth.
In her gasp he grabs the swords
then throws them into the crowd.
Now they need her no longer–
they can kill for themselves,
and not one by one as she did,
but in hundreds, thousands at once.

She still waits on the shore
just beyond the reach of waves
in the tangle of weeds caught
on the farthest jut of rock.
She waits for someone
tired enough, and so grown wise,
to bring back her swords
and clothe her again with awe
so people at last can die
as they were born,
each, one at a time.

FIVE

He is red stone
up from the center of the earth–
crystal lines shining
countless angled surfaces
polished smooth into one,
curved into head and arms
into thick body and striding legs.

He is red stone
the red of his life-blood hard
the red of his life-fire cold
as he wanders across the lands
with the red of sunrise,
moving westward every hour
never waiting for the day.

He reaches one hand
up into the sun
and it is gold to the wrist,
the golden fingers splayed
with the flash of raybursts
dazzling between them,
calling up great birds
to swim in the splash of light,
to spread their feathers
into fingers and hands,
into wingèd minds,
into messages:
to be touched
not seen,
to be grasped
not heard,
to be held
not known.

The wheel-hub always turning,
he circles the world
upon the ever whirling rim.
Red with the sunrise,
he reaches his hand
into golden minds.

Midnight Noon

ONE

Their eyes guess at her body
within the skin of cloth
that shapes around her movements
as she walks, as she breathes.
They see the sliding curve of thigh
the pointing breast
as if the weave of threads
were spun by glass spiders.
Their eyes linger over these scanning lines
until their tightened throats swallow dry.
Then they see her looking into them,
realize she knows their want,
is saying a wordless
Yes
before they can even plan
a first lie.

Her eyes, their eyes
seeing only eyes:
flash-point eyes
black centers open
reflecting instantaneously–
reflecting only eyes
bind-blinding eyes-to-eyes
back-forth back-forth back-forth–
finally fused.

They think they are stalkers,
have netted her and brought her down,
that they will slit and flay,
drink her into their thirst.
These are the ones filled with fear
of who they might yet have to be,
who cannot let themselves see
anyone but themselves–
the ones who must possess
or be the nothings of someone else.
But it is she who searched for them,
found and snared them.
And now she draws them.

She pulls them into her,
takes their groans and sweat,
makes their inside bodies so wild with her
they will never find another
able to reach into their bones.
And when they try to remember her
and the feel of themselves in her
it will only be a feel of fragments
and only in fall-apart daytime dreams.

She has them.
She pushes them away.
She keeps their inside bodies.
Day-on-week-on-month she grows great,
then slivers to the dark of the moon,
birthing her lightless children
into the night spaces
between the careless stars.

The silent children wait until
the time for her to send them
down into winter rivers
black between snow banks.
They run clear and cold,
hungry for their drowning fathers
who come at last–
tired of trying to remember,
tired of feeling fragments,
tired of less and less.

TWO

Whenever the moon is full two nights running
the day caught in between
is one forgotten.
The sun wanders up and down its horizons
and she returns from the hunt
to roam the shore.
She sees him there–
clothes scattered over the sand,
his skin hot
but ready to shiver bumpy
in a chill breeze
or a first touch.

Every double-moon day he is there
and she comes to share
his smile
his breath
his pulse–
all melting her flesh into blood,
into warmth and laughter.
Each time she returns
she knows he remembers the whole of her,

with his eyes somehow
absorbing her light image
into all he is
yet every time is still becoming.
They lie back in the sand,
so soft and giving when they move
yet hard rock earth when they stay still.
Eyes closed into each other,
they hear their inner words
in the blue lapping of the water.
And she forgets all those others
and all her dark star-space children.

For this day at least
there is no hunting or trapping,
at last no need or want.
They sleep into the chant of the sea
reaching up around them:
longing, belonging
longing, belonging.

Each year she hides away
her double-moon child
in the fire of the sun,
safe from the lightless children of her nights.
In the infinity of years
there will be an infinity of children
in the night spaces,
in the sun days,
an infinity of drowning winter river fathers,
an infinity of laughing magic oceanic fathers.
Yet even she cannot guess
what the becoming will be
when all infinities converge
—as they must—
into that solitary point
when the moon dark and the dazzle sun
become midnight noon.

Sun Dog, Moon Dog

ONE

A handbreadth before sliding
around behind the earth,
a hot afternoon sun
blazed upon me
as I wandered a summer road.
With one sun dog
glow-barking in the north,
radiance called to me:
    Come run with us,
    be our south dog,
    the dog on our right.
    Come hunt with us,
    see our prey-world
    laid out for the kill.

A high hawk wheeling
slips across the sun,
wing feathers fanned out
the spread fingers of a hand
playing the air.
In a prism moment
splayed feather filaments
catch the ray-burst.
I look through it,
the sacred sun-flash below,
and through the hawk-eye disk
circle searching
    light, light,
    shade, shade–
the brights and darks
running the surface earth
as sun and dogs hunt,
with blind fire dazzle eyes.

Then panting and pounding
    I stop,
the north dog prance-dancing to me.
I stand against the sun
at its red horizon,
my skin bronze gilded,
and I cast an endless shadow
back over the raced land.

I absorb my sun
in an infinitesimal eclipse
almost lost in my crown.
The thin wedge I am,
pointed without dimension
into the light,
seizing those few wave rays
into my thickness,
I become light-speed voided shadow
racing across universes.

Star shadow,
    nothing
becoming ever less,
an everlasting infinite
coning out from point
more and more blurring–
    the only Always
after suns have died emptied
at the end of the hunt.

Growing outwards
always greater–
After light-speed ceased
I am the bounding dog
happily yapping into forever.

TWO

Night before dawning
black-purple still,
double pathlights waver over ocean
drawing down moon and moon dog
filled, thieving-white, from the sun.
They urge inside me:
　Come rise with us,
　be our south dog,
　the dog on our right.
　Come swim into us,
　see our dark world
　ready to wake.

While whales breathe
the ocean rolls at rest
listening to fistsize blowhole gales—
red blood purpled black
now glutted with a whole skyfull
and backs hump-arch,
heads plunge down,
tail flukes soar in torrents
then beat into the depths.
They sound a thousand fathoms
within the sightless dark
singing to titanic ships
crewed by soggy bones
(hard when they first gulped water,
now womb-soft, ghosting away).
　Then up, up
tunneling through the sea
breaching into the night
cratering reflected moons and dogs
　and me.

In my moon dog water path
ripples glint–
    black spots
    flash spots–
and I shine shadowless
flowing within the currents.

I sense sea sand hands
fingering my skin
as I lie in the shallows
    quickened,
    born.
I become the quiet,
moving in lived mystery–
a swell of waves
over upper layers,
an eddy of sea river
bounded by water banks.

And I float awake.

I shiver away swimming dreams
of moons and dogs
as I feel the shimmer of you
happily lapping here near.

    A sun dog
    gone out all alone,
    as shadow echoing
    worlds that end.

    A moon dog
    grown into all one,
    the I-and-I Eternity
    always now-in-now.

Rocking

Half the time Ol' Granny rocked,
the other half she did things.
She never seemed to sleep,
she winked in her rocker.
She was a big bulk woman,
so she was folds of skin
none stretched tight,
just layered and slabbed.

She rocked a lifetime,
miles enough back and forth
to go around the earth
out to the sun
up even to the stars.
But only her head went anywhere–
all yellow-white
with some crazy hairs
not caught in the knot.
Back, forth
squeak, squawk
Ol' Gran in her rocker clock
bobbing away miles in time,
her two feet unmoving
pressed against the floor.

She laughed to herself
thinking of her feet
tied inside her shoes.
Special shoes.
Old, falling apart,
bound up by black electric tape.
Her electric shoes–
could take those bump bone feet
everywhere in her flying machine.

She was born in her house.
Her Grampa had cleared the land
and built it from his trees.
Ol' Gran
her Grampa
back to the Indians
back to the Tower of Babel
when people first came here–
That was her title deed
to the posts and beams,
creaky boards and horsehair plaster,
the deed of the poor
who had to do for themselves
with whatever was at hand,
who could never finish.

Long ago her Dad had found
odd wallpaper rolls.
Rooms began with one
then turned the corner with another;
part way down the hall
it all ran out.
He patched his Pa's plaster,
she patched his patches,
but the cracks still came
and ceilings bulged down.
Orange tulips, green leaves, brown garlands
were all scuffed together
in the kitchen linoleum
in front of the sink and stove
and under the table
where boots had ground it grey.

When she was young her Dad was old,
her Ma had gone up to the Sky
leaving them all behind
to live as best they could,
and somehow they tricked
stony dirt to grow things.

From all those young years
she only remembered the Christmases.
In the front room
with its three wallpapers
they had a fresh-cut tree,
nothing on it,
but with the sharp smell
of the deep woods in winter.
Beneath the tree was their present:
a big box filled with puppies,
puppies to play with
to lug around
to talk to
puppies tumbling over each other,
lunging to lick-kiss faces,
hugged asleep with children in the huge bed.

She remembered Christmases
and the weeks after.
One by one the puppies went.
Wandered off down the county road,
her Dad always said.
And every week after Christmas
they had a rabbit stew.
So she learned what Christmas meant.

But one year there was a puppy
like no other puppy ever born.
Hers forever!
After she hid him in the woods
how did she keep from smiling
as she told her Dad he must have
wandered off down the county road?
She fed him through the winter
and he grew up half wild.
She would see him
when he came to the tree edge
and his eyes glowed red in the dark.

One by one over the years
her brothers and sisters
wandered off down the county road
like Christmas puppies.
But she knew
she could live forever
if she chose.

So she rocked and did things,
roaming everywhere in her electric shoes,
winking bits of sleep
when she would see
the red glow eyes
and know:
Mine forever!

The Heart Collector

Two slams of the hammer
and the nail was in snug.
When he swung
every muscle and tendon popped
up and down his arm,
reaching across his back,
over his chest,
right to his feet.
With those two slams
he pounded himself into the wood
along with the steel nail.

He was in there
in the bones of the house
until it fell down or burnt up.
He liked that–
to be in all sorts of places
and no one even knew,
to be inside where they lived
and no one could get him out!

This was one of his secrets.
Everything else he learned
growing up with his father–
wood and tools and women.
That's what his father liked.

His father loved only him.

When yer-Maw-the-Squaw was around
I thought she was really somethin'.
But I learned.
I may be slow
But I can learn.
She taught me two things:
How to get me the best kid in the world
and how to have him all to myself—
right after you came along
and she took off.

He was the best kid in the world
who just came along one day
sort of out of nowhere.
He never had a mother,
never knew her name;
his father never spoke it—
she was always
yer-Maw-the-Squaw,
nothing more.
He knew she was not a real Indian.
Yer-Maw-the-Squaw
was a name for a nobody,
who trailed behind for a while
then disappeared.

Names are important—
no name, a nobody,
simple as that.
He was Jack,
his father was Johnny
and he always called him Johnny,
never Dad or Pop,
because Johnny was somebody.
And he was always Jack,
never Son or Boy or anything,
because Jack was somebody too.

Never forget:
always call people by their names.
They eat it up.
And they're right!
If they're high up on the totem pole
then add the Mister or Doctor;
that's part of their name,
that's who they are—
or think they are.

There was one set of Names
Johnny never said out loud,
never
even if he whacked himself with a hammer.
He'd come out with every word
for every part of your body
and what you could do with it.
But never one of the Names.
Jack learned this from the beginning.

How would you like it—?
every other grunt was your name,
every cuss was your name,
and all strung together
with enough raw words
to blow the seat out of a outhouse!

All the Reverends keep yellin':
Don't do this, don't do that,
thou shalt nots
or thou shalt not get to Heaven.

Everybody gets to Heaven,
but then the fun begins.
Just imagine—
you used to say one of the Names,
and there HE is!

You'd be so scared
you'd wet your pants.
But the nice people up there
would all pretend they didn't notice.
That would make it worse even;
now you'd be so ashamed
you'd start to bawl.
Water comin' out of both ends—
that's what Hell is!
Makin' yourself into a nobody.

You can do whatever you want,
good or bad,
right up 'till you die.
He'll forget it all.
But you can't never forget
if you made Him a nothin'.
There you are forever
in the middle of your puddle.
No fire, no pitchforks,
just slobberin' wet,
and all the nice people
takin' care not to look.

Jack never said one of the Names,
and he loved Johnny
as Johnny loved him.
But way down inside he hurt
whenever he thought how he looked.
His face was fine
and his build was good.
It was the bone in his chest
where his ribs joined.
It was in backwards or something,
so there was a hole
like someone smashed into him
and nearly killed him.

Johnny said not to worry,
just a weird bone
bent the wrong way.
Lots of people must have them.
But his weird bent-bone chest
was the only one he ever saw.

Maybe somebody did smash into me,
nearly kill me–
maybe yer-Maw-the-Squaw
before she went off.
Maybe she didn't go off at all.
Maybe Johnny killed her
for smashin' into me.
That could be why
he never says those Names:
insurance for up in Heaven
to make sure HE forgets
all the good and bad,
like killin' yer-Maw-the-Squaw.

But when he looked at Johnny
he knew: No!
she ran off,
left him alive
with his inside-out chest.
So he was born that way;
must be a reason why.

He studied himself in the mirror,
even though it hurt,
and after a while he realized
he had two faces:
one on his head
another on his chest.

The hole was a nose
but pressed in instead of out.
His two nipples were eyes
set up high on the squares,
not down at the corners.
So the face on his chest
had an odd look on it—
like it was always asking
"...And?"

A face on his chest,
that was part of the puzzle.
He never told Johnny.
This was his first secret
and he knew nobody could understand,
not even someone who loves you.
Then came the second secret.

> Wham!
> Staring straight at me
> on this poster of Mexico.
> A statue from a temple—
> he was laid out on his back
> propped on his elbows
> with his knees up
> and his neck and head up.
> And on his middle
> there was this big bowl.
> But it was his face
> staring straight at me...
> It was my face,
> my chest face.
> Same funny look.

Chac Moòl
who collects living hearts
from screaming Aztec altars
and brings them to the gods.
Jack the Chac–
same face,
same bowl in his chest.
Then the hurt stopped.
Yer-Maw-the-Squaw
ran away because she saw
the empty bowl
waiting for her heart
she was afraid to give.
But Johnny gave.

Jack the Chac–
I go around buildin' houses
and buildin' myself in
so they'll be somethin' special–
This House Built By The Heart Collector.

That's how I make a livin'.
But it's not why.
I'm out to get every heart I can.
It's easy–
I smile,
and say their names,
and give them my special look.
Then one of these days
I'll go up to Heaven
with my bowl loaded
and give them all to Him.

And He'll say somethin' like:
Why, it's just what I wanted!

Then I'll flash my Chac face
right at Him and say:
"...And?"

Kali

Over at the crossroads
about a mile or so,
best food in the county.
A flagpole outside
with a red-check tablecloth
flapping away night and day.
White letters over the door:
    Calico Callie's.

Funny place though,
a long wood cowshed–
used to be cows,
pure-breds the old man had.
Stalls fixed into booths
with the kitchen to the back.
Hung along on the walls
sepia pictures of cows,
the prize ones with names–
    Cleopatra
    Queen Elizabeth
    Empress Josephine–
all standing four legs solid
with their snouts sort of up,
and state fair rosette ribbons
stuck on their horns.

Wood sign outside
tells you what you get.
Always the same, no choice:
    Coffee & Pie
    Cannibal Stew.
No tea, no beer, no fizzy water.
Coffee like nowhere else.

Callie warns newcomers:
    Drink it straight down,
    no swishing it around
    if a dentist made your teeth!
And all kinds of pie,
a different one every day–
but never apple:
    Get mom to make you apple pie,
    that's what moms are for!

The coffee and pies are great;
come just for them.
But cannibal stew,
now that's what Callie is all about.
You sit down at a wood table
with hell-hot coffee in your mug
and a quarter of pie on your plate.
Then comes this thick steamy stew
in a white crockery bowl
with a round spoon stuck in it.
    Here y'are–
    cannibal stew–
    nobody goes to waste!

Callie has this idea about people:
Everybody is always eating everybody else.
    You die;
    the worms and bugs get you;
    you go up into grass.
    If you die in Africa, say,
    you're some gazelle's lunch.
    Then you and the gazelle
    are a lion's supper
    and maybe buzzard dessert too.

Over here it's more likely cows,
or it could be sheep.
So you're a rack of lamb
or a side of beef.
Here at Calico Callie's you're stew.
So it's cannibal stew!

Of course you never know who's the stew.
By this time everybody everywhere
must be pretty well spread around
in and out of all the eating
all over the world millions of years.
Maybe that's why the sepia pictures
hung up around the walls,
the prize cows Callie's Pa used to have–
Cleopatra
Queen Elizabeth
Empress Josephine.
You eat your stew,
drink your coffee,
finish off your pie.
You look up at the pictures
and around at everybody.
Makes you think respectful,
and feel kind of good inside,
almost.

Getting Born

He wondered what he'd like to be
once he got out of his mother.

A rock, maybe.
No—too big,
even a pebble, too big.
To get born,
squeezed out—
A grain of sand!
Small enough;
then what?

Loll on the seashore
watching the tides
move the ocean around,
then swim in the surf
with the other grains,
all of us together
growing smaller and smaller
and older and older.

Till it's time
to find someone
and beget something.
Find an oyster
and have a pearl.
Become a pearl!
And hang from a rich lady's ear
or sit in a ring on her finger.

Live in a warm velvet box,
only come out for parties
or when she meets somebody secret
and knows I won't tell.

Then one day when I'm bored
with what she always does
I'll slip away,
hide where she can't find me
even if she looks right at me.

I'll wait for someone else,
someone who'll sell everything
just to have me,
who'll look at me
for hours and hours
and smile because I got born.

That's what he thought
still inside his mother
wondering what he'd want to be,

when she pushed hard...

Eye Child

I heard my mother
whisper to my brother:
  Stop staring at the colored lady.
Seated with us everyday folk
in the clanky streetcar–
  Where was she?
  All purple or green
  or somesuch marvelous color–
So I never noticed
the smokey mocha woman
big and warm next to me,
smiling the mother-smile.

She knows all there is
about babies and children.
She watches their eyes.
She sees newborn eyes,
squint slits still dark inside
from months of swimming.
She sees eyes and mouths slowly open
in the embrace of breast
to feel and see
the round moist moon
colored deep from the heart.
Then they see her eyes
looking into their eyes,
the back-forth
looking-counterlooking
eye-reflecting-eye.
And they smile.

They grow with looking,
reaching out to touch and take.
They begin to see-speak the world
and look into other eyes
for the yes-and-no signs
that tell them the truth.
When they tell their first lie,
because they fear or desire
or want their little lives to seem big,
she laughs them back to the truth
and their eyes again grow soft.

Yet she knows the soft return
of eye-reflecting-eye
can cease.
She can see it as it happens
the first time the lie is real
and there is no laughing way back.
In the feeding moon of her breast
she feels the sigh
rising for them
as they look away.

But she is ever searching
for eyes which have caught sight
of the ones inside other eyes,
and cannot look away.
She is always at that moment
when eyes are in delight.
To these she gives her power,
the power to come forth
from within their eyes
and freely be who they are,
unshielded, uncovered,
out where everyone can see.

She watched my eyes
back then when I looked around
to discover the wondrous woman
all purple or green.
She blessed my eyes with power:
I see the marvel of people
and cannot look away.
She blessed me in her mother-smile
that day I failed to find her,
the warm smokey mocha woman
there in my brother's stare.

Sacred Goats

Our family altars glowed
with worshipful ancestors,
men and women strong in virtue
travelers of oceans and continents
builders of towns and homes.
In the shadows of our shrines
some others lurked
evoked every now and then,
sad salutary figures to transcend.
In my growing up
Grandma was our priestess,
and when she spoke the names
of the goats among our sheep
it was always in formularies,
terse words of warning.

Great Uncle James ran off with a squaw!

Grandma had no prejudices,
she especially admired Indians,
but as noble children of nature.
Great Uncle James' sin
was a wife outside kith-and-kin.
We always married cousins
or friends-of-the-family,
no one beyond the clan–
so you knew what you got!
We had no Red Indians.

From the first I loved
Great Uncle James and Great Aunt Squaw.
It was my secret sacrilege–
Grandma should have known
the way little boys think.

I would lie awake in bed
and shape their images.
He was dressed all in black:
a frock coat and stovepipe hat,
with the rumpled dignity
of an Honest Abe.
And he was running,
running away with his squaw
arm in arm across the plains,
and she in her buckskins
all dangle-fringed,
in a red and yellow blanket
with a bright feather in her hair,
hair black as his hat.
I never knew her name,
Great Aunt Squaw was enough—
We did have a Red Indian in the family!

Great Uncle Will drank himself to death!

If I loved Great Uncle James,
Great Uncle Will inspired awe.
When I daydreamed him
he was always in our basement
seated on the cement floor
surrounded by brown glass flasks
ranked in neat rows
all in easy reach.
Imagine: drinking so much so fast
you drowned!

One day when everyone was busy
I took my unbreakable bakelite cup,
wrapped a towel around me
and filled the sink.
I watched the water rise
within the white porcelain
set on a stubby column
topped with an acanthus capital.

(My Dad said it was Classical,
the only thing our ancestors saved
when Vesuvius blew and buried Pompeii!)
The tap spouts were fish snouts
and the nub spoked handles were enamel
blue for cold, red for hot.
But underneath the pipes crisscrossed
so the right water
would come out the right tap.
(My Dad said that was Classical too,
the work of a left-handed plumber.)

I stood on a box at the sink
and scooped up cold water
in my unbreakable cup
and drank as fast as I could
gulping and gulping.
I never finished
and never drowned.
My amazing Great Uncle Will
drank himself to death–
he must have practiced for years!

I always wonder why.

Lazarus Again

The afternoon they buried his body
Judge Hester returned.
They were all there in his house:
the Governor and Honorable Justices,
Senators and all the rest,
paying last respects.

Suddenly silenced they turned,
and there he was at the door–
high color in his cheeks,
curly white hair everywhichway
and the always smiling eyes.
A nod of greeting but no word,
a loving glance to his wife,
and he was gone.

A hundred saw him,
the worthiest witnesses;
they set it all down
under their hands and seals,
then went on home.
        Damnedest thing!
        Makes you think!
But hardly any did.
They went on home,
back to what they were doing.

He had been the eldest of eight,
his seven brothers ministers,
fire-and-brimstone circuit riders
like their ferocious father before them.
That man had been a Denouncer,
right out of the Bible,
emptying vials of wrath
all over the heads of the ungodly.

Judge Hester had a metal picture:
Old Matthias,
his seven reverend sons,
their seven righteous wives.
He kept that picture at hand–
to remind himself: I escaped!
Old Matthias never forgave him,
never forgave anyone–

> Once he was set on by Indians,
> scalped and left for dead.
> He got to a settlement
> but they were afraid
> and turned him away.
> Somehow he recovered
> and first thing went back
> to denounce the ungodly–
> They were promptly wiped out
> man, woman and child.
> Old Matthias said: Amen!

The eldest son went off
to see where Indiana was.
There he married Martha,
begat three girls and a boy
and began to serve the Law.
He met God in Indiana too.

> Strangest man I ever knew–
> Johnny Appleseed Chapman.
> Planted trees all over the place
> wherever settlers might come;
> the apples would be waiting
> and they'd know someone did it,
> a free gift,
> and they'd bless God.

He planted apple trees for God
so people could see Him
as He is: Gift.
He also gave people books,
huge books full of visions.
Emanuel Swedenborg saw them:
the New Jerusalem here on earth
built by love,
and all the kinds of wisdom
you could find in everything
if you learned how to look,
and the signs and symbols
in all the Bibles
so you could form His Mind
inside your own.

Then he heard about California
while the fighting was still on.
He sold house and land
packed everything up
and set off in a wagon train.
Before they left though
he and son Will
made a last visit
to the silent monks,
their mystical friends
down in Kentucky.

One of the monks gave Will
a string of brown seed beads
with a little gold cross at the end.
He told Will it was prayers,
the prayers of the monks
to take with us West,
prayers you could hold in your hand:
Seeds, for our life on the land,
Cross, for God in our lives.

A dozen dozen wagons,
wheels wearing ruts in the earth
across plains and mountains
to the wall edge of the Ocean–
And every night at camping
Judge Hester read by lantern light
from his great Polyglot Bible
and a book of Swedenborg's visions
laid out on the wagon tailgate:
the Table of the Lord's Presence
in the Tabernacle crossing the wilderness.
Each day Will walked the miles,
the string of seeds in his pocket
gently nudging against him
with the prayers he could touch.

Judge Hester loved Law-work.
He hated judging.
Golden Jerusalem was still unfinished–
there would have to be judging
and he would have to do it
in the violent land of California gold.
He dreaded the final act of Law
yet he would command it.

> But I have a special pen for it:
> a black ebony pen
> to remind myself every time
> how awful a thing it is,
> to remind myself to take care
> not to become fire-and-brimstone righteous
> and imagine God wills it so.

He had another pen,
gold with a golden topaz top.
With this he wrote down his visions,
all the wonderful ways he saw:
God is Love
and he wrote down his wisdom,
all the times people showed him
there is one command and only one:
Little children, love one another.
He could see all this
even when he had to write
with the black ebony pen.

One day Judge Hester took cold and died.
And there he was
beyond all imagining,
where apple trees and Bibles,
golden pens and brown seed beads,
where every vision there ever was
and all the wisdom that ever could be
were hardly even hints of hints of hints.
He seemed to hear a far off voice–

Send someone back to tell them...

They have had Moses and the Prophets...

But, someone from the dead...

China Girl

Once upon a time
—a hundred years ago—
in an ancient city
by the Western Ocean
—in wooden San Francisco
  before the Quake and Fire—
an ivory maiden dwelt
in a humble home,
the beloved of her father
—a Chinagirl lived
  in a Chinatown flat,
  a daughter, not a son.—
There had been brothers
but they were dead;
so all her father's love
now was hers alone:
he must not die sonless,
she must bear a boy
to reverence and remember him.

One midweek day
on her way to market
a bolting horse
spooked by the wind
struck her down.
She started to drown
in the blood flooding her,
and her life,
life for her father,
began to breathe away.
But a blue-eyed giant of a man
caught her up,
carried her off
to a place of healing peace.

There her father and uncle came
to buy her from the foreign devil–
he had saved her life,
she now was his.
They offered the price
for the priceless child:
not coins– coins buy things–
but a soft yellow-gold ring
embossed with blossoms,
the hope of seeds.

They brought her back to Chinatown
to a Chinaman husband,
and she grew old young.
Her womb sagged from sons,
her full breasts drained flat.
Her eyes dimmed within deep creases,
she thinned and wrinkled into paper
until one night she slept away.

Her father never knew
he had bargained with a wizard
who took the gold flowered ring
but charmed the girl,
smiling silent words
spell-binding her
within its circle–
he kept the Chinagirl:
the smooth ivory face
and dark eyes loving,
forever alive in the sorcery ring.

At length the wily wizard
gave the ring to his son
who gave it in turn to his,
the once-upon-a-time Chinagirl
living happily-ever-after
even now,
golden around my finger.

Tiger Bed

Great-grandfather believed it:
a man and woman bouncing
in a tiger stripe maple bed
bounce out baby boys.
It was one of his Principles:
Tiger beds get tiger boys.
Great-grandfather had a tiger bed
and begot a tribe of sons.

For each the Principle held,
the marriage gift was a tiger bed,
and his sons begot sons.
Oh, there was a sprinkling of girls,
but count back the months:
parents off visiting!
Tiger beds always get tiger boys.

When tigers run
everything they are moves,
hidden under their stripes.
No muscles show,
all simply flow.
As tigers lope
their padded paws
        WHump
                whump, whump
                        whuMP–

No wonder tiger beds bounce boys!

I was bounced from this tiger bed.
High headboard scrolling back,
lower footboard curved away.
Both shimmering with stripes
black-orange, harsh orange-black
dizzily all over.
I lie flat and look up–
the tops and bottoms of my eyes
jump with stripes
against the creamy ceiling–
like looking up the white fur belly
of the tiger wife who bore me.

Tiger men seek out tiger women.
Tiger and tigress:
each fully alive within,
each with night caught in golden eyes,
each rough-breathing a purr delight.

Tigress-mother and mother-woman
both alike in their young
giving lives in blood and milk.
Neither cub nor I remember
but we have the taste,
and when we lie still
we feel the pulse.

As I lie here quietly
where I began
I see wooden rib stripes
and almost remember:
I was once inside.

The Heedless Monkey

Old men have small boxes
for keeping leftover things–
cigar boxes, wood or metal boxes,
but never round tin cake boxes–
the boxes must have hard corners
and proper hinged lids.

Grandpa had a wooden box
the color of adobe clay,
stamped all over with gold designs
and curlicue letters spelling
CIGARILLOS SUPREMOS,
and a naked Indian lady
lounging on the seashore
smoking a cigar.

He kept this old-man-box
in the drawer of a tall chest
with his collars and handkerchiefs
and all his dress-up stuff.
When he took out the box
and opened the lid
there was an incense smell
of soft-grained wood and glue
mixed with long ago delights.
It dreamed of domes and towers
and palm trees on the seashore
where the naked lady smoked her cigars.

The box was filled with odds and ends.
There was a pocket knife with a broken blade–
        Still cuts on the edge.
One of a pair of cufflinks–
        The other might show up.
A round watch with one hand–
        You can always guess at the hour.

There were also important doo-dads.
A locket with a curl of baby hair—
        To prove I used to have some here.
The sabre-curved tooth of a boar—
        The better to eat you with, my dear.
And then there was the monkey,
a little soapstone statue
with the head broken off—
        Somebody in China carved it
        and you can see how he did it
        because parts and angles are still left on.
        They paid him two or three cents for each
        so he carved them quick,
        made as many as he could
        as fast as he could.

I used to think about that Chinaman,
his slant eyes squinting tired
as he carved out monkeys all day,
carved this very monkey—
I wondered if he planned it,
made this one some special way
so the head would break off,
then Grandpa would find it
and put it in his box.

There are three kinds of monkeys:
hands over eyes,
hands over ears,
hands over mouth.
This is the fourth kind:
no hands, no head.
The other three say:
see, hear, speak no evil.
This one says:
fear no evil.
The others are wise,
and this might be the wisest one
or maybe the dumbest of all!

Never see, hear, speak, fear–
the headless handless monkey,
Grandpa kept that heedless monkey
in his naked-lady-box
just in case.

The Quick Brown Fox

The last words she heard:
  –Ready...one...two...three!–
Then the click blink of the black box
and she was forever on the shiny side
of the thick paper
that always curls backwards.

Each year or so she came across it,
and paused to look again.
There she was beside that gorgeous car–
a running board to step up on,
the polished body tall and square
(you could get in standing up,
practically walk in)
spoked wheels, chrome bowl headlights.
She stood there smiling in the early afternoon.

And that hat, a real one–
iridescent feathers tight against velvet,
the whole cap pulled down over flat curls
edging out under the brim.

And the chinese beads strung on a gilt chain,
dangling double all the way down
with a carved jade charm at the loop
(good luck, long life, or something).

And the silk dress light in the slight breeze,
pastel stockings going up somewhere underneath,
pointed shoes with a strap and pearl button.
And the fox.

After a while whenever she saw that picture
her stare fixed on that fox,
the warm fur circling her shoulders–
everything hanging down loose:
the full tail with its white tip,
the boneless legs,
the paws without claws,
and the head.

That head–
hard nose, no jaw
no brain, no skull
pointed earflaps, no ears.
But it had eyes, glinting glass eyes
orange brown with black centers
never closed, never asleep–
eyes that glared
always about to bite.

She grew old,
looking at herself in that early afternoon
wearing the feather velvet hat
standing by the wonderful car.
She could never find a way to warn herself
about the fox, the murderous fox,
which slyly lay around her neck
and slowly stole her life away.

The White Whale

ONE

I alone am escaped to tell–

1
Alone–all one.
I am one,
the only one,
and so must be that one
who is all there is;
alone escaping
all escaping with me,
escaped to tell
someone
everyone
myself.

To tell a secret,
to tell over its words
like telling over beads,
little biddings all strung together–
seemingly little
but one after another
into a loop circle
never ending
never broken.

Telling all the words of the secret
no one wants to hear,
cannot bear hearing–
Which must be why
I alone am escaped,
to tell myself the words
tell the secret out loud
so I cannot escape hearing,
until, telling it again and again,
I finally believe.

2

Two words begin it:
dark
light–

No man can ever feel
his own identity aright
except his eyes be closed;
as if darkness
were indeed the proper element
of our essence,
though light
be more congenial
to our clayey part.

So this is why
no one wants to hear:
we must go into the dark
to recognize,
not by seeing
but feeling,
though not by touching
but doing,
some sort of creating
inside, deep
–where it might be too deep.

Light and seeing:
the surfaces, the outsides
and just being that way.

Or in the closed-eyes Dark:
making it happen.

3
Eyes closed,
there is another fear
in that inner dark:
not knowing what might happen
now outside in the light,
might take hold of my clay,
reshape it.
But to tell the secret
eyes must be closed,
all light sight cease.

Suddenly, the feel inside:
a new creature.
A wonderful new thing
within me,
but as I feel it
how small it seems,
wonderful but small.
Is that all I am?

Another moment of the secret–

> *All noble things are touched with*
> *melancholy.*

To be small inside,
not infinite.
To remember seeing outside,
seeing a universe
starting from me
from my center,
a solid unbroken stretch
of parts and pieces
all fitted together
out in all directions
wherever I looked.

But I am small inside,
can feel nothing else
and starve to be more.

This too is the secret–

> *What he ate*
> *did not so much relieve his hunger,*
> *as to keep it immortal in him.*

4
So I keep eyes closed,
search deeper into my ocean;
always for so much more–
senses of measure vanish.
Here without tides or currents
the universe above,
whatever its size,
means nothing.

TWO

1
Closed eyes can open,
yet even if closed again
I know the lure to look
will draw me up
back into the light–
the clay part of me
and my own identity
insist together,
at least for now.

Up on the moving surface
of my unmoved ocean
a wooden ship speaks
with the slap of waves
with whaler sailor voices
with the dull thud
of a fake leg
as an Ahab paces the deck
back and forth forever
on the endless hunt
for the stalking monster.

Ahab—a puzzle name.
Two syllables together,
two ancient words joined:
Brother, Father.
The brother of a father.
The brother of one who begets—
the other who does not beget.

This Ahab—mine,
scar gashed up and down his body,
half dismembered,
a whale-ivory post
strapped to the stump of leg—

moody stricken Ahab
with a crucifixion
in his face

2
This is the one
out in the sunlight
crisscrossing the surface
of my unmoved ocean,
the clayey part
unidentifiable,
never begetting
insatiably demanding—

that certain sultanism of brain—
incarnate in an irresistible dictatorship.

Lifeless but not dead,
ever seeking
but eyes never closed
so ever seeking
something out there,
whatever it is,
the monster that maims
but stops short of the kill:
the white whale
that watches the hunters
with its tiny eye,
disinterested
unless they come too close.

3
My torn apart Ahab
saw into that eye
once, for a moment—

All visible objects are but pasteboard masks.
But in each event—
in the living act, the undoubted deed—
there, some unknown but still reasoning thing
puts forth the moldings of its features
from behind the unreasoning mask.
If man will strike,
strike through the mask!

That inscrutable thing
is chiefly what I hate;
and be the white whale agent,
or be the white whale principal,
I will wreak that hate upon him.

I'd strike the sun if it insulted me.
For could the sun do that,
then I could do the other—

4
But there is another of me
listening on that ship—
With my clay Ahab,
the brother of a father,
is the father of a brother.
Wherever the one is
the other must be as well:
Father's brother,
Brother's father.

Up on the surface of my ocean
carried within that ship
I am both of these,
both lifeless and life giver.
As Ahab thumps the deck
and I curse my monster
I am also at the masthead
as high as I can climb,
and stand above spray stained sails
as I search the line
shearing air from water
for an invisible whale.

The last of the secret—

There is no life in thee now,
except that rocking life
imparted by a gentle rolling ship;
by her,
borrowed from the sea;
by the sea,
from the inscrutable tides of God.

5

Eyes opened or closed,
seeking outward in the light
for things
or feeling in the inner dark
for myself–
no longer important.

From someplace
someone is speaking about me
but also to me
all at the same instant–

> *the blending cadence*
> *of waves with thoughts,*
> *at last he loses his identity;*
> *takes the mystic ocean at his feet*
> *for the visible image of that*
> *deep, blue, bottomless soul,*
> *pervading mankind and nature.*

After Twilight

In the dry almost hot afternoon
she waits for the last train.
She is old,
great grandmother old,
slave Africa old.
Her face is her eyes
which have seen everything
and wish to see nothing more.

A fine silk dress
gathers her in soft folds
of a blue reflected in the sea
the first minutes of twilight
after west sun has let go
and water wavers away
eastward toward dark.
On her head a turban hat
pointed high in front
of the same oceanic blue
with a wisp of black veil,
hints of starless night.

The train comes without tracks
down the crazy Main Street
which undulates almost into hills,
a black-top sprawl
without sidewalks or set edges
nearly a block-apart wide.

The train is four huge cars
the size of houses
on monster wheels
running all askew.

Ashy salamander boys
cling easily belly-down
to the steep peak roofs,
happily beating the dirty canvas
that covers the boards
with the flats of their hands,
to puff out billowed dusts
that make the train go,
to the sound of thudding blows
in a slack drum head.

As the train comes into view
the townsfolk begin to hum–
a single note
at first unnoticeable.
The single note divides
into two, then four
and the chord moves up and down,
spreads and contracts
following the undulation
of the hilly street
and the cloudy train.

She boards without looking
and the people turn away
as the laughing little boys
set to their banging again,
and the last train leaves.

The people stare past each other
but see everyone sideways.
Too late they realize
someone got off the train.
A giant is among them
striding down the alley they empty
as they part in fear.
They are left unharmed
as he passes in great strides,

but they have all seen
he is wrapped
in the dark eclipse
of some other planet.

At the far end of Main Street
he comes to the foot of a hill
circled from bottom to top
with winding intersected streets
all lined with shabby buildings.
As he starts up
the street becomes wet
with a previous rain.

The higher he goes
the deeper the water
which does not flow down,
but towards the top is so deep
he must begin to swim.
In the now swirling current
hundreds of soft fish cascade by
colored dappled coral-and-white,
ovals, rounded bars, or waves.
He swims back down with them
to where the water shallows,
so he stands and wades
to step out again
onto the dry street below.

There the people hum once more
singing to the undulating pavement,
singing for a train to come.
They cannot believe
the last train was the last.
They will not believe
the old lady took
the final twilight with her,
and now the giant
is among them forever.

Earth: Last Day

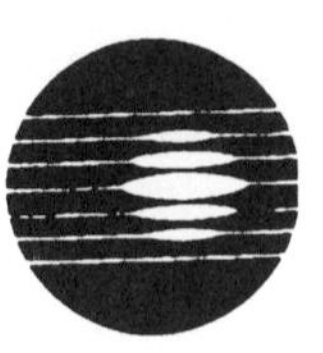

ONE

The hour before Saturday dawn
we reach the Dark Town
in the mud coast steam.
They are waiting
and bow low
as our salt-wet feet
bless their single street.

They guide us past
the slave steps
where men and women
are shown for sale.
We do not look,
we do not listen
to the bargaining.
We are as unseeing
and silent
as the merchandise,
who could not care
who bought them—
until long, long after.

The buyers ignore us
so intent are they
fingering bare flesh,
figuring the sweat
for ox-work
or pleasure.
Discreetly off to the side
the Temple treasurers
fail to recognize us
as they decide the tithe
the slavers are to pay:

the flawless one-in-ten
found altar-worthy
to sweat blood.

We do not pause,
there is no time.
No matter:
they will buy and sell
drain and kill each other
to the end.
And of course it is
the end that calls us
to the Dark Town
for that Saturday dawn.

No one really lives
in this flowerless town.
The slaves are brought
from lands along the sea.
The buyers come down river
when the slavers light the fires
signaling their wares are here.
No one knows where the Temples are
or how many there might be
or who or what Powers
eat and drink at their altars.

The one long street
leads from the water edge
up past the slave steps
and off towards the east.
Marsh muds stretch away
from each side of the paving blocks
and breathe a fever stench
of night fog and day haze.
The lone straight street
sends us to the coming sun.

There at the final paving block
are the two chanters
who sing up the sun each day.
Without them
earth would still turn,
sun would still seem to rise.
But without them
the sun would rise old
slowly cooling, slowly dimming.

The chanters are deep bronzed
a beautiful man, beautiful woman,
always seated quiet
except for those few moments,
the time it takes for sun-up—
from the first tip glare
till the lower curve of the disk
clears the day horizon.

Every sunrise they chant:
as they sing their touch,
as they tight embrace,
as they catch new light,
as they frenzy in love.
And every sunrise flares young,
hot with what still might be,
bright gold in the sheen of their bronze.

We come up behind them
as they stare to the east
lips just about to part.
But before the sound,
before first sun fire,
we reach around them
silently slit their throats.

At last—
there is no sunsong.
The blessed withering begins.

TWO

It is always weeks
before the Temple slaves
grow to know
they are free.
No one tells them.
They are left unbound
to wander the sanctuaries
and come upon the tables
set for their feasting.
After wary days they realize
they find no altars
awaiting their terror.

Then one by one
they discover the jars,
stone cylinders tall and cold
set row upon row
in the cool of a columned hall.
In the quiet they listen,
hear faint scratching sounds
first in one, then another,
this one silent,
that one sighing.
The scratchings cease
then some other begins again,
and again responses scatter
up and down the rows,
the jars talking, saying things
but not in words—
in the inner irritations
within the tubes of ears,
itching the hairs in there,
insisting.

Slowly each is taught
the trick of the Temple tithe,
the men and women saved,
those few among slaves
who do not wish to own.
None could make
the slavers set them free,
but every slaver honors gods
greedy for the blood
of the one-in-ten—
gods just like themselves
grabbing, squeezing,
throwing away,
seizing more, the best.
Back in the Dark Town
the Temple treasurers always choose
the very ones the slavers want—
so slavers always believe.

THREE

At the outermost lip of the world well
dwell ever sleepless lionesses,
hard and unbreathing beasts
of black stone smoothed soft
by a thousand thousand thousand
hammer blows,
chiseled from living rock
carved round on its flat face,
then pried loose from the high relief
to be forever only half—
half the head, one eye and ear,
half the hungering teeth
set in a half mouth jaw,
and claws fixed and flexed
in half the paws fore and hind.

The lionesses prowl
among stunted unleafed branches
of half trees hewn from the same black stone
with trunks reaching down the well
through earth-center and on,
on out into the vanishing point
of the universe root.
Half, always half,
never Nothing–
half of half of half.
The half-blind lionesses see to it.

FOUR

So long since chanters ceased
singing up the sun,
since slaves heard the jars
and found themselves unbound–

Now it happens:
How, trapped in thickets
or hours asleep
deep in moss forests,
the arrested force
burns loose, runs wild,
wanders lost as smoke
clouding the sky around,
tearing eye-blinks,
blackening char.
Ash powder
hot, warm, cool, cold
blowing over,
blown off
from a cinder sun,

another new dark giant
among the dying live stars,
light radiant,
flying into nowhere.

All those tithed free
cannot care—
Other earths and suns,
other songs at sunrise
in endless half-life time
clutched in the claws
of the half-lie lions.

Ragnarök

his voice *her voice*

1
Cold,
these seeming years

these winter years,

colder
even after dawn and sun;

winter now,
always only winter.

We lie here

side by side,

awake asleep

open eyes not looking
at the ceiling

aware of every crack

of shadows shifting slowly
through a dull-star day,

then staring long into the dark
the next winter night

seeing the empty cold
above us.

2

They put us here
before the end,
before their last day,

to start over,
the new beginning

to breed the race again–
children, future children.

But we remember,

we remember them
putting us here

killing us alive
for their children–

children of rage

or of laughter,

of war

or of peace,

murderers

or lovers.

No matter.
We remember.

They all died
that last day.
There will be no children.

3

We lie unmoving

arms touching,

my right your left

my left your right,

the outer round of shoulder

the outer swell of forearm,

the back of our wrists

the bone back of hands

to the knuckles;

our fingers cupped
and turned away

turned back to ourselves,

not ever intertwined.

We may never stir,

ceaselessly stare at
the day ceiling

at the night dark,

feel only the outer
curve of our arms,

the backs of our
turned away hands,

as winter deepens
around us,

the ever colder
sunrise sunset,

as we sleep awake

just touching–

Warm. So warm.

Dreams with Truth

ONE

Poking through winter woods
with the feel of dry leaves
under a crunch of first snow,
a thin iced crust
an inch at most–
This-year leaves still hard
wait to soften again,
but not green again:
to soften dark into earth,
with the new green to come
up on the lost branches.

Ahead, beyond this roofless hall
of tree columns and pillars
and spindly sapling poles:
a bare open space,
white snow circle around
a black disk of pond.

A quarry sliced deep into layered rock,
split off chunks hauled free
cut and chipped into squared blocks,
sent out to almost anywhere
to be fitted together
as sort of tortoise carapaces
armouring a prey world
of soft flesh bodies.

Left behind empty
a stone hole of fracture veins
that bleed a seep of water
filling and molding itself
to what used to be here
but now is something else
somewhere else.

TWO

I stand here at the edge,
look into the surface
to see myself inside there
looking back at me,
unimpressed.
There is a sky above me
down there behind me.
I see that dark sky
but not the real one
the blue one.
That other of me can see no sky,
not without me shifting our eyes.
If I do
we disappear.

This is a surface game:
looking, and looking away;
doubling myself pretending;
seeing more dimensions
than I would even need;
playing with the dark
safely in the light.

But deep within the quarry hole,
emptied of hard stone shapes
now filled with rained down ocean
taking any empty shape,
so much deeper than the two of me,
there are dreams,
my dreams,
dreams with truth–
not just haphazard sparks
wandering asleep in brain,
pieces of unfinished thinking,
convulsions of my unfinished living.

Dreams with truth, real truth
like the real sky up behind me
that I cannot see without turning,
the blue sky my unreal reflection
cannot see either, without ceasing.

Dreams of truth
happen all the time, every night.
All those dreams are true–
just my mind in different shapes,
shapes tumbled together,
not in neat lines of daytime.

Dreams with truth
happen only here
in the daylight dark quarry pond
as I look and see sky
my unseeing self does not.
My seeing is dream,
unseeing is truth.
Dreams with truth–
all I am,
all of me bound up in that
With.

THREE

To be naked together,
absolutely naked,
no rings or things
no colors or scents,
nothing but skin and hair
finger nails, toe nails,
all forty of them.

Excitement!
Ourselves just as we are,
living bodies alive together!
Freedom,
absolutely mad freedom!

But she says:
Oh that,
Everybody feels that—

So.
She cannot see it,
that real sky behind me.
I should have realized,
remembered
who her eyes are.

So.
I must dream it
feel it all by myself,
feel the excitement.

But now we are too close,
skin-to-skin.
No matter what we look like,
looked like a moment ago:
we are too close to see
anything but eyes.

Keep your eyes open!

But she will not.

I close mine too
and we disappear.
But not the excitement,
not the truth
or the dream.

FOUR

Half a year beyond,
all the quarry stone
has been built into
a hollow cube
hundreds of people high–
a pool of invisible air
rising up away from surfaces.

The inside walls are bare,
great blocks dressed smooth,
joined, almost seamless,
a vast empty space
readied for us to happen.

We are always ready
to come here,
to be emptied
of what we used to see–
At any moment
unprepared
though we know it can occur.

A yearning to hold
something, someone–
not merely see reflections
but to feel in our hands,
hands cupped and closing around,
enclosing into ourselves
at least partly.

Here in this open space
measured to the size
of hundreds of us
it is designed to happen.
A mood of melancholy,
but not sad–
the empty is waiting,
simply waiting,
what will happen still unknown.
It must be.
Not just another reflection,
just more of me
endlessly multiplied.

FIVE

There they are again
he and she
and still naked, as always–
they have never been covered,
do not even know
what that might mean
or what it could feel like.
But they are older,
more than the half-year
distant from the pool.
They are alive in a different way–
not just the surface image now.

They sit near each other
but face in opposite directions:
he looks northward
she toward the south.
They turn their heads
to see each other
in the rising east
in the setting west.

He stretches out his hand to her.
            I reach for you.
She takes his hand in hers.
            I feel the warmth of touch.

Her eyes are grey;
in shifts of light the grey
that can be green or violet.
She tells him with her eyes:
            Never trust me.
            You reach for me.
            I might not be here.

I smile back at you:
            I know.
            The pool taught me–
            It is my hand stretched to touch.

There is a wonderful silence
in my new dreaming–
seeing images, then
seeing through the images,
transparencies
receding rapidly behind me
in the vanishing empty space
more and more filled with us.
Reaching touching hands create
out of nothing.
So eyes and what they say
mean nothing.

But I keep looking, wanting to see.
A part of me will always trust
the grey eyes not there anymore.
The rest of me knows better.

SIX

It is winter,
the best time for looking,
for trees are leafless
so the earth is bared.
But more than a naked skin–
a skeleton, stripped bones:
rocks humped in snow,
weed tangled stubble twigs.

There is great loneliness in it,
like being out too long
on the sunless cold of an iced lake–
the sort of round ache and snaking pain
that slides inside
but never numbs.

Winter loneliness is the waiting.
Though earth is bare
and everything seems to show
something is hidden,
waiting to be seen.
The need to look–
but not into the pool
to see only surface again,
not into her eyes
to see her gone again.

The need to look
and find something so simple,
so everyday commonplace,
an unimagined universe
must be lurking there.
Outwait winter bare bones
until the skeletons begin to move
fleshed out with my own images–
images, not mere reflections,

images, thousands of them
caught in the thousand lenses
of eyes of insects.
Images of me as I am
sucked into their pinpoint brains
to become electric shocks
that shout to their nerves:
                    jump and fly and skitter away
                    fast fast–
The genesis of my universe,
the cosmic bang of me
out into everywhere.

In my universe
everyone, everything breathes
but not air into lungs.
They are all made
of whatever I am
so they are alive
my way.

I dream.
All I do is dream,
dream with truth
the past I have not lived
a future I will not live.

I leave behind a quarry hole
to fill with something,
all my images rushing off
to be built into something,
where some man and woman
will sit near each other.
He will reach out his hand,
she will take it in hers.
He will look into her eyes,
see they are the grey
that could be violet or green.
And he will wait.

The Three of Them

The three of them–
the man, the woman and the other–
picked their way
up across the ridge.
On both steep sides below
rose the huge trees
with their dense smell of green–
their own sharp needle green
and the soft greens of mosses
in the creases of bark
and the rocks that weigh down roots.

The man was the first to see it,
perched on the swaying
tip point of a tree.
The woman sang to it
the incense chants of the cavern fires.
The other reached out to it
with a sky hand to draw it in.
But it could not be tempted back.

Yet at odd times it would remember,
and whenever it did
the chant words would live for a moment,
and the man would suddenly see again,
and the other would touch someone
with the power of night skies
and dreaming.